DIGGING UP DINOSAUR FOSSILS IN

AFRICA

Little Mitchie
an imprint of Mitchell Lane

Creating Young Nonfiction Readers

Little Mitchie lets children delve into nonfiction at beginning reading levels. Young readers are introduced to new concepts, facts, ideas, and vocabulary.

Tips for Reading Nonfiction with Young Readers

Talk about Nonfiction

Begin by explaining that nonfiction books give us information that is true. The book will be organized around a specific topic or idea, and we may learn new facts through reading.

Look at the Parts

Most nonfiction books have helpful features. Our *Little Mitchie* titles include color photographs and graphic aids, a table of contents, a glossary, and an index. Share the purpose of these features with your reader.

Color Photos and Graphic Aids

A lot of information can be found by "reading" photos, charts, maps, and other graphic aids found within nonfiction texts. Help your reader learn more about the different ways information can be displayed.

Table of Contents

Located at the front of the book, this list shows the big ideas within the text and the page numbers where they can be found.

Glossary

Located at the back of the book, the glossary defines key words and phrases that are related to the topic. These words and phrases can be found in the text in colored type.

Index

Located at the back of the book, an index is an alphabetical list of topics and the page numbers where they can be found.

With a little help and guidance about reading nonfiction, you can feel good about introducing a young reader to the world of *Little Mitchie* nonfiction books.

Mitchell Lane
PUBLISHERS

2001 SW 31st Avenue
Hallandale, FL 33009
www.mitchelllanepub.com

Little Mitchie

First Edition, 2025.

Author: Meg Greve
Designer: Rhea Magaro
Editor: Madison Greve

Names/credits:
Title: Digging Up Dinosaur Fossils in Africa / by Meg Greve
Description: Hallandale, FL : Mitchell Lane Publishers, [2025]

Series: Digging Up Dinosaur Fossils
Library bound ISBN: 979-8-89260-237-2
Paperback ISBN: 979-8-89260-415-4
eBook ISBN: 979-8-89260-249-5

Little Mitchie is an imprint of Mitchell Lane Publishers.

PHOTO CREDITS
Alamy: Universal Images Group North America LLC/DeAgostini, 10-11; MasPix, 16-17; Stocktrek Images, Inc., 18-19; Shutterstock: Michael Rosskothen, cover, 1; Colorcocktail, cover, 1 (sign); Herschel Hoffmeyer, 3; Aust28, 4, 6, 9, 11, 13, 15, 17, 18, 20, 23; Noiel, 5; Mahmoud Hassan, 6-7; Daniel Eskridge, 8-9; Catmando, 12-13; Catmando, 14-15; Frame Stock Footage, 20-21

CONTENTS

When Dinosaurs Ruled the Land

The air is hot and dry in some places. In others, it is warm and humid. Dinosaurs big and small live and rule in all the different climates in this area. This was Africa before it was a **continent.** This was the time of the dinosaurs!

Before there were seven continents, all land formed one giant continent called Pangea.

Paleontologists have found it difficult to discover dinosaur **fossils** in Africa. But what they have found help tell a story of Africa, 200 million years ago. Let's learn about some African dinosaurs!

DINO DETAILS:
Some dinosaurs had wide, flat tails. Paleontologists think these may have been used for swimming or hunting in the water.

MEAT FOR DINNER? MEET THE CARNIVORES!

Spinosaurus is one of the largest dinosaurs ever discovered. It had a long sail on its back. It also had a tail that looked like a paddle. Spinosaurus may have been able to swim!

DINO DETAILS:
Some dinosaurs probably looked more like lizards than beasts. But they were still fearsome hunters!

Euparkeria was a tiny **predator** with sharp, curved teeth for eating bugs and dead animals. When it was chasing its **prey**, it would run on its back legs.

DINO DETAILS:
Dinosaurs that hunted in the water used long, curved claws like fishing hooks to catch prey.

Suchomimus looked a little bit like a crocodile. It had a long snout with many sharp teeth. Curved claws allowed this **carnivore** to hook fish from the water.

DINO DETAILS:
Some dinosaurs laid their eggs and raised their babies in nests. Giraffatitan laid her eggs while walking and did not care for her young.

More Plants for the Herbivores, Please!

Giraffatitan stood more than 50 feet (16 meters) tall! It had a small head with sharp teeth used for munching on the leaves of tall trees. Like most **herbivores**, it lived in groups of three to six.

DINO DETAILS:
Some dinosaurs were so small, they may have looked more like housepets than terrifying monsters.

Lesothosaurus ran fast with its long back legs. Its body was small and light, making it easy to run from predators. Lesothosaurus had a beak that helped it break down food.

Heterodontosaurus had three different types of teeth! It even had tusks that may have been used for protection. Heterodontosaurus used its long tail for balance while running.

DINO DETAILS:
Paleontologists believe that some dinosaurs may have had a mane of feathers.

Millions of years ago, Africa sat right in the middle of all the land on Earth. It was home to dinosaurs of all shapes and sizes. By studying African dinosaur fossils, we can better understand the earth's history and the world we live in today.

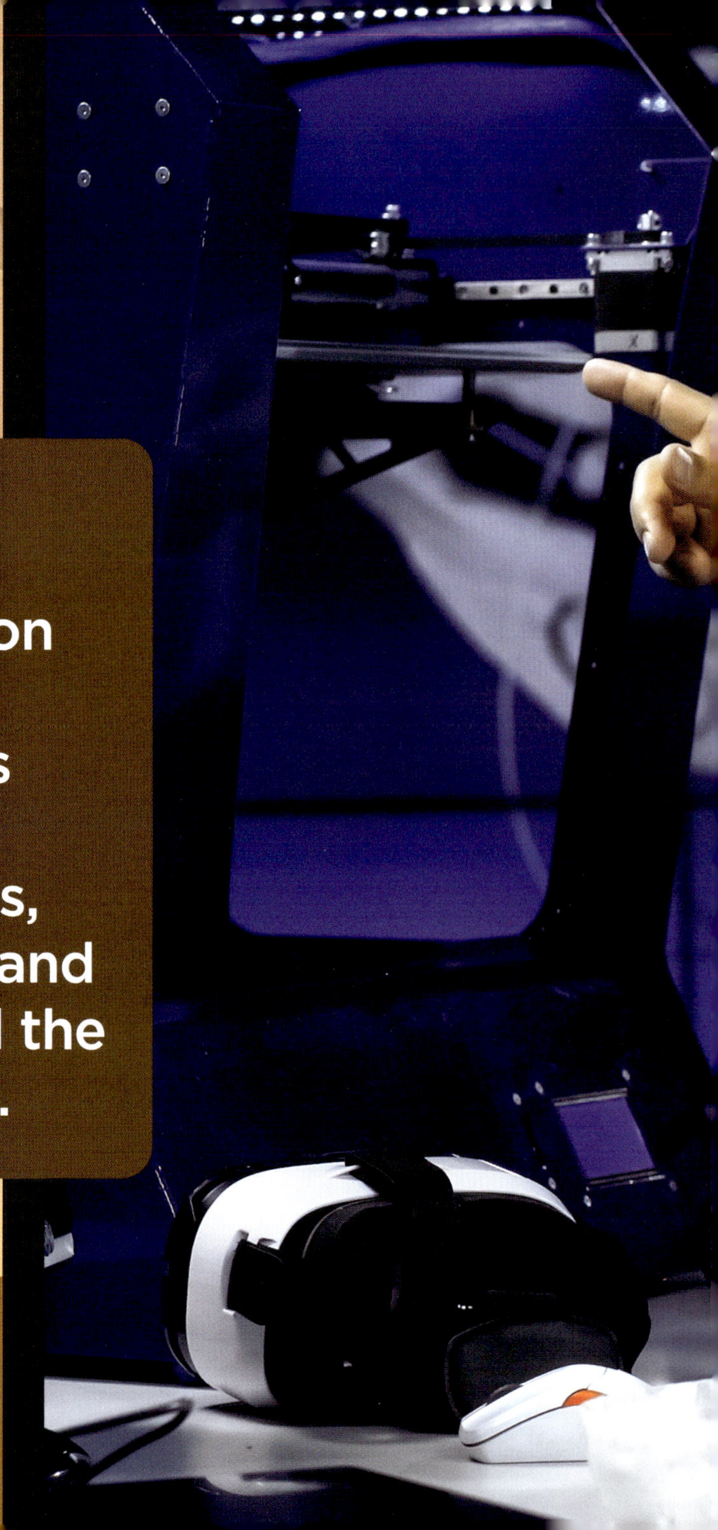

Where Did the Dinosaurs Live?

Not many dinosaur fossils have been discovered in Africa. But there are still plenty to learn from!

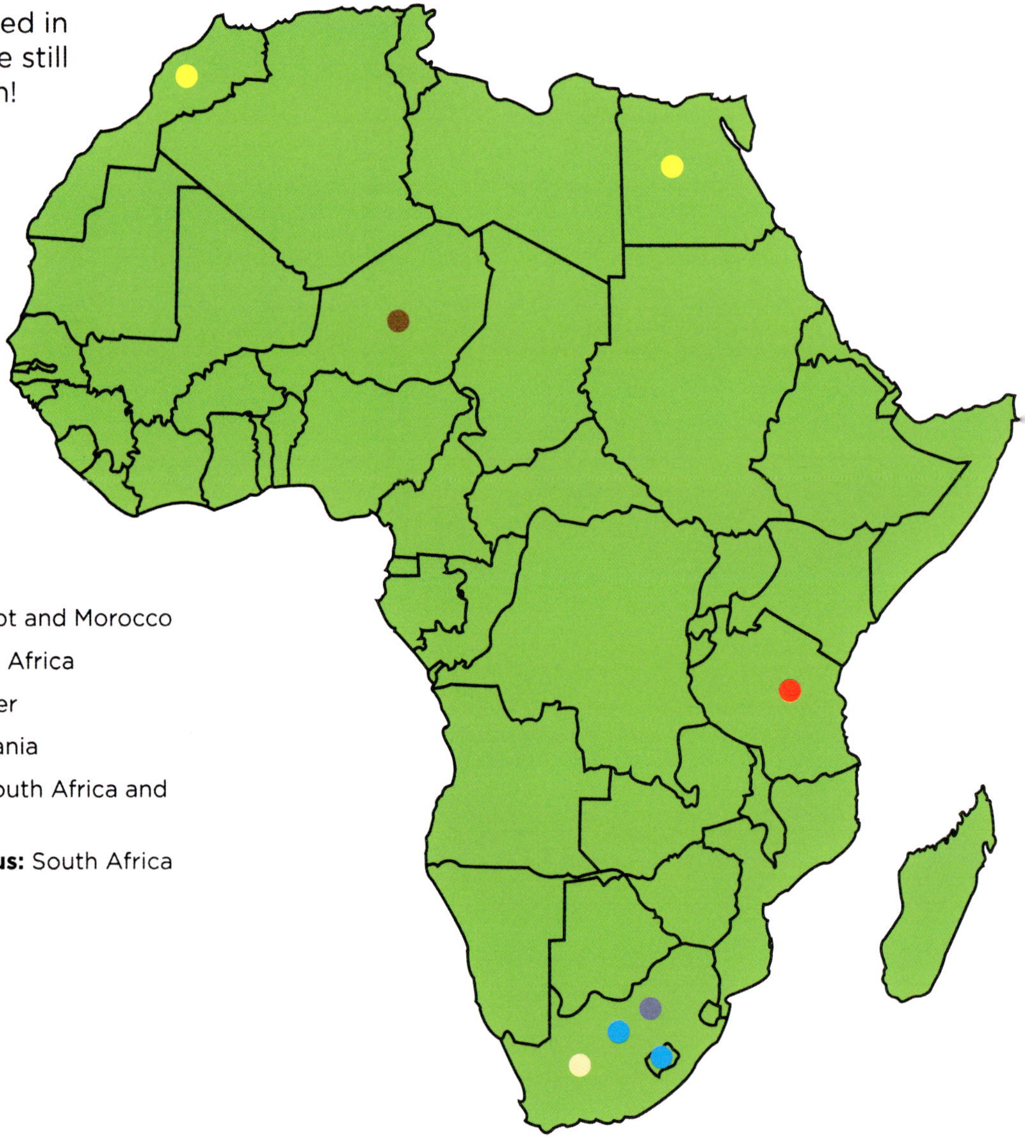

- **Spinosaurus:** Egypt and Morocco
- **Euparkeria:** South Africa
- **Suchomimus:** Niger
- **Giraffatitan:** Tanzania
- **Lesothosaurus:** South Africa and Lesotho
- **Heterodontosaurus:** South Africa

Interesting Facts

- The word dinosaur means "terrible lizard."
- Many dinosaurs may have been covered in feathers.
- About 66 million years ago, a huge asteroid crashed into Earth that killed off all dinosaurs except for birds.
- Today's birds are related to dinosaurs.
- Dinosaurs first appeared on Earth about 252 million years ago.

Spotlight On: Alfred Brown

Alfred Brown was born in England but spent much of his life in South Africa. He was a teacher, librarian, and paleontologist. He is famous for finding and naming more than 21 new kinds of reptiles and dinosaurs. He studied living reptiles, collected more than 2,000 books, and never stopped learning. The people who lived around him called him "Gogga," which means small insect. Brown also collected and studied plant fossils. Not only was he interested in fossils found on Earth, he also enjoyed observing and studying the skies.

Glossary

carnivore (KAR-ni-vor):
A meat-eating animal

continent (KON-tin-ent):
One of the seven largest pieces of land on Earth

fossils (FAH-suhls):
Rock that forms after a living thing is preserved in the earth

herbivore (ER-buh-vor):
A plant-eating animal

predator (PRE-duh-ter):
An animal that hunts other animals for food

prey (pray):
Animals hunted and eaten by other animals

Index

Further Reading

Barker, Chris Dr. and Riley Black. *Dinosaur Knowledge Genius!*. Dallas, TX: Brown Books Publishing Group, 2021.

Chinsamy-Turan, Anusuya. *Dinosaurs of Africa*. Cape Town, South Africa: Penguin Random House South Africa, 2022.

Hansen, Grace. *Dinosaur Graveyards in Africa*. Minneapolis, MN: Abdo Books, 2021.

On the Internet

Meet Some Deadly Dinos!
https://www.natgeokids.com/uk/discover/animals/prehistoric-animals/meet-some-deadly-dinos
Learn lots of facts about dinosaurs that lived all over the world.

Dinosaurs: Tour a Dinosaur Lab
https://sciencetrek.org/topics/dinosaurs
Watch a tour of a dinosaur lab and learn facts about dinosaurs.